Clean

Also by Kate Northrop

Back Through Interruption
Things Are Disappearing Here

Clean

Poems

Kate Northrop

A Karen & Michael Braziller Book

Persea Books / New York

Persea Books, Inc.
277 Broadway, Suite 708
New York, NY 10007

Library of Congress Cataloging-in-Publication Data
Northrop, Kate, 1969–
Clean : poems / Kate Northrop.
        p. cm.
"A Karen & Michael Braziller Book."
ISBN: 978-0-89255-367-9 (original trade pbk. : alk. paper)
I. Title.
PS3614.O78C57 2011
811'.6—dc22
                        2010053694

Designed by Rita Lascaro

FIRST EDITION

Printed in the United States of America

to Nick Ingram

Contents

I

Cat

Now do you see what I mean?
In the woods how the headlights'
Beams ride over trees' leaves
Without seeing or meeting them.

It's how you walk through the field
Without entering the field
Or how one reads one's own name
Closed, as a window.

But we must find our cat now
And search with a flashlight
Hoping the beam and cat match.
Here we call *here* walking around

Shrub so dense the moonlight
When the moon is full
Slides over it evenly neatly
Then is still, as the surface of a spill.

Like the Girl in the Car

you are tired, tired, and like her you are sure

that specifics in the world only dirty the world

because isn't the park littered like that? Condoms,
the sidewalk. And crushed therefore with mint? The ducks

still gliding by, their orange feet tucked in
and trailing like the corners of ties

stuck out of suitcases. And such costumes! Here come children

from the movies, from Mars, children from the moon—
But like the girl in the car you are tired

and do not want to be seen, or stopped

like a little figure in the middle of a replica village. You want
if anything to be seen through, not the blaze

or the lingering arsonist, but the crowd gathering, each face

turned one way, and clean, as the first idea of a freeway—

Evening

Then the yard we knew around us
Rose around us.

Then the yellow walnuts
Blue and stripped by wind

Grew taller, darker, like pop-ups
In a children's pop-up book, although the sky—brilliant
Electric—was not as we'd hoped,

Was not a reader's eye
Floating over us

So that I saw the garden that evening in the future,
The garden through the humid air:

The fence lined again with roses
Joey's Rose, Calamity—each pale

And filling with light, a lamp
In a window. *But listen, hey*—
You'd touched my knee

And when I looked back, the garden

Was still as a scene
At the bottom of a globe

After snow has settled. I saw
It was at heart a document.
Perfect, swept

As other documents.

Iowa

You imagined yourself
There on the overpass
Leaning through snow
Farther toward cars

Their outlines still dark
Their headlights
Locked by distance
Then opening as if

Cautiously the beams
Lengthening over the median
Onto leaves the underside
Of certain leaves

And the drivers inside
Each face described
By shadow each
Finally simple the skin

Lit by the vehicle's instruments
In the glow of the dash
The faces you'd dreamed of
Then gone beneath you

Leaning over the highway
Farther toward cars
Toward headlights
Opening in the snow

Clean Houses

As in a mirror
Your face steadily there
The magic of a clean house is
It is and will not appear

No one can see into it
Although the chair is here
The rug is here yet it
Resists, does not appear

Even family framed in photos
Something's always gone
Something's left to which
You cannot respond

Children, say, or their shadows
Gathered by a lake
What was the name
Canandaigua? And then that's clear

As a refrain is clear
Rising toward you who listen
Closely in houses
That do not appear

Stray

Four days he circled, his fur
matted with mud-sludge and thick beneath

with burrs we imagined

tight against his skin, though he moved
each night, farther in: mornings, his prints

(the mud dried within
here and there, into tiny peaks) marked

the steps of the porch

then the porch itself, until
in daylight, we'd look up

and he'd be there, sitting

beside some farm object—truck,
white lilac, compost heap—

erect as a question
though calm, direct, like a tourist
posing by a monument, hands

folded quietly, neatly dressed.

Night Snow

Slight hiss, as a canoe
Pulled back over grass

And the flakes
Widening where they slip
Into patio stones, that place

Dark as a small lake
Closing over at the edge of the yard.
Nights like this,

The necklace on the dresser
Pools there, glitters

Clean as the detail
Remembered in dreams, though still
It is a guilt gift

And glitters, and pools there
So the names, the faces
Drawn through names,

Rise in the night snow
Often and light the yard.

Late Aubade

Early October,
Snow over the meadow

The campsite we'd made
At the end of summer
Was somewhere there

Though I never promised,
Did not say I'd return
One way or another

To the Snowy Range,
To the farthest lake: still, black
As a mirror back,

And the entrances closed.
I never said anything

As someone standing in a corridor
Says nothing in a corridor

Or I shifted: near, close

In the Snow

Now there's a man in the distance
And you are driving the car

Now he is in the distance
No bag beside him no car

And you see he is complete
As a knock as a dog's bark

But belonging only to himself
In the empty road in the snow

Now there's a man in the distance
And you are driving the car

II

Winter Prairie

Around which the houses darken
And the windows surface silver-pale,

Around which the ditchwater
Freezes stunned in a ditch,

The water like the windows: clear,
Secretive. One knows

A window: it gives everything away,
Nothing back. One knows

The TV light scattered through,
Blue, cold, though not as blue, not as cold

As the prairie, the winter prairie, spare
And so clean it becomes like this

A struck note, a shape
Cut from the world yet held in the world

—like staring hard into a grave.
I speak to you; clearly someone else speaks.

Night Drive

Shoulderless mostly, old
This is the road
You should not be driving

Not at night, at zero
Or well below,
Bone-stark, so cold

Each turn appears
As a figure in a dream
Sure, demanding:

Look, fields are rising—
And they are, the bright
Snow-stripped fields,

Like a shroud
Or a female voice
You never loved me

And that's true
Even the farthest homes
Close enough

To your home
Where often in the dark
Downstairs in the kitchen

The beams of headlights
Moving through the room
Moved through you

Caldera

Now the crater is a lake
And pines rise around it, homes
Beneath the pines.

First it's aloof, sweet in moonlight

Then it shifts at dawn, mist-thick
Like too much wine.

And it's not so far to the other side

That you couldn't see a fire
From anywhere around it,

Couldn't quickly swim it,

Though once inside
You are slowed
In a hold so steep

There are no sides there
Nothing to climb out on

And farther down's
Impossibly long, the length of a dream,

From which the cold
Draws into you a note

Low enough the body
Will not pronounce it. No,

No, it won't.

Night

Again it is night
Which takes up the mountains
And takes the pale roads in.

It is night again, goodbye, there go
Mailboxes, driveways, there go the white cords
Of lights neighbors left in the pines.

Goodbye, goodbye, it is night
Outlining the farthest house,
Taking up that house

So in the emptiness
When the moon comes out
It floats our lawn; the lawn floats

And the garden returns,
Clear as a voice you knew,
Someone you once loved, a sound

Both warmer now and cold

The Film

Come, let's go in.
The ticket-taker
has shyly grinned
and it's almost time,
Lovely One.
Let's go in.

The wind tonight's too wild.
The sky too deep,
too thin. Already it's time.
The lights have dimmed.
Come, Loveliest.
Let's go in

and know these bodies
we do not have to own, passing
quietly as dreams, as snow.
Already leaves are falling
and music begins.
Lovely One,

It's time.
Let's go in.

The Lake in Moonlight

Now a bird cries around it

Now the boats and leaves
Drawn into the border
Speak back from the border

And the paths falling through laurel
Rise from

Now a bird cries around it
And the stairs to the house,

Driven in, metallic,

Shiver and gleam—the world's
So tale-telling—though not

This wind you remember

Returning to the shore
Long after it's been closed

Aspens

You would say they are white
They are not white
And their secret is
A private cleanliness

You would say the sound
Their leaves make is slight
It is not slight the sound
Of the leaves is the sound

Of very small stones
Rolled under the tide
A sound that keeps you awake
On certain nights haunted

As if on a back stair
Or here at the window
Drawn again by the meadow
Thin transparent cold

III

Detail

Fifteen years and still she hardly speaks of him, your uncle
who died on the linoleum, overdosed on heroin, or of the linoleum itself,
oddly shining, swept

When I am near to the sea
I think of the sea

Like an argument practiced in one's head
The sea goes over itself
You could say this, say that

But there's never a way out
Because the sea rhymes everything

———

When I am near to the sea
I think of the sea

The meaning is between

Yet everyday in the basement, throwing darts at the dartboard.
A thud as the tip strikes cork but moments before and you swear that already
you've felt this time, it bites in

Entering the room I heard something

Entering their kitchen, I was unexpected—the sunlight
Falling across the wall

Rippling like a swell
From a very distant boat

I heard such a commotion. Noises in the next room:
Tap, tap, *shit*, tap

Most women are always going to look a lot better than you.
That's because they will have outfits.

So exquisite so you knew before it ended
It would never be enough

But other sounds heard in the world
Can be satisfying: acceleration
After shifting into third, the squeak

Of a paper towel as you clean
A streak from the glass

And so you also do not make a habit of discussing

Your dislike for the retarded, for the curdled eyes of the blind
Or for the eyes the deeply drunk,

Unable to focus, head bobbing, their speech almost a lowing, almost
    bovine

How a line drawn in a sketch
Is the curve first of a shoulder
        Then just a mark again, a line

—

Traffic, seen from the sky

—

How snow falling into the lower field
Then is the lower field

What you want to remember
You write down on sticky notes. "Return shirt! Flight."

The first day they had to write down
Three things they loved, three
They hated

Loved: pulling moss from the seams
Between bricks; Jell-O, how when touched
With a spoon, it resists

Hated: a too-severe part
In someone's hair, visible scalp;
The skin formed on house paint;

White condiments

(Miracle whip, tartar sauce, mayonnaise)

Sometimes you will want to break things

At one point I could remember her

Mary by the Swings, in first grade

In the first grade, she was blonde
She had a long face for a girl

It was the beginning of fall
And the other girls, under the window,
Gather around her

Even then at that moment
She was the image of something—
Like a painting, or a barn

Seen out a car window.
Perfect, remote. An other.

Sometimes you will want to break things

Learning of a lie,
There's nothing quite like it.

Finding out someone's lied
Sends all sailing away

Or it collapses it, in slow motion
Like a tent onto the ground

(Although finding out a lie
Also confirms. All you thought was true
Is true.)

———

My father for example
Was an excellent liar.

The trick to falling asleep is to keep from getting too excited
When finally you start to fall asleep, to keep from getting too eager

When the world begins to unhinge

But I don't want my poems
To be like Bukowski poems

I don't want to write
Cock-and-Beer Fart
Beauty poems

Here's-the-Truth poems

The list of things you don't do! Don't fly fish, don't speak Italian, don't give dinners. You don't play guitar, run marathons, mountain bike, don't go mushrooming on a lovely autumn day. Don't like live music. Don't know anything about anime. Don't write your dreams down, don't sew, knit, weave, sing, have children. Don't draw.

Other people are much more interesting than you.

But I think everyone wants to be found out

When we all found out
X was sleeping with Y

We thought of all the times she said

Just the other day
this guy and I from marketing were saying,
my friend and I were saying

———————

And the language of lying
Is the language of escape

You *get away with it* or you
get caught in a lie. You get
tangled up in your own lies

You *walk right into it*
As in, Liar: *I went to Carolina's with Cheryl last night.*
Lied To: *Carolina's is closed on Sunday*

And there you are

You know not everything always has to be life or death

Still, the poems shouldn't be precious

Like posing for yourself in a mirror
To see if you look alright

You could no more write that poem than motorcycle to the moon—

Afterwards no one spoke of it.

It shouldn't matter.
Why should it continue to matter?

It's just a sordid moment
From one life

As little and sordid as my life.

Because I am my father's daughter.

Outside the maples click to red
And the whole autumn business is over

Before you know it.

Sometimes you will want to break things

When I was waitressing:

A square of sunlight
On the corner of the table, on a pack of cigarettes
The sound of a fork against a plate

A car would pull across the gravel of the parking lot

And I'd feel, or hear, a ringing

The list of things you worry about is long and absurd

I had a friend in Iowa
Who lied all the time. Whether he said

We went water-skiing
or *I listen to James Brown a lot*
It was all the same

Like those t-shirts Bill once made
White t-shirts, printed in black:

Je n'existe pas

The guy who lied
You couldn't place him,

You couldn't imagine

Where he was

Try to be clear about it

   . . . to loosen with all ten fingers held wide and limber
   And lift up a patch, dark green, the kind for lining
        cemetery baskets . . .
   That was moss-gathering.

But it isn't enough, not really—

Sometimes I can find what I've lost
By imagining where I was recently with the lost thing

I put my sunglasses up on the top of my head
Like this, in the computer section at Staples
And I already called Staples

I set them down
On the end-table at Julie's
And I already called Julie

I didn't have them this morning
When I went to the gym

Walking from the car, I had to squint,

The sun was so bright

You never could hold a note

. . . As if I had broken the natural order of things in that
   swampland;
Disturbed some rhythm, old and of vast importance,
By pulling off flesh from the living planet;
As if I had committed, against the whole scheme of life, a
   desecration.

IV

Skating

                    I

        —into the air! But one doesn't enjoy, I don't enjoy

watching the turns they skirt the edges of
then leap from

or watching their gestures limited to joy
        —always a reunion

or longing, which is wounded, love-

sick. Or entering their twists, their double
        axels, how they smile, smile . . . each muscle

staking the smile down. Clearly
        there's no room there —for them

in the performance, a mimicry

        responding not to ice
but to noise, the audience. And we eat them up!

                    II

Therefore in the course of the performance, one skater may suggest
        that now it's long ago

and soulful, hasn't she come awake

in this special place, somewhere
        hidden, beyond a stand of trees.

III

But still it's a sickness, to smile to be so pleasing,

so done-up in iridescence, weird
as photos of wedding cakes. And it's odd

to learn routines so thoroughly the body

leans into them, even off the ice,
     walking through the kitchen, down the hall

     —like a car pulling to the right

Though it's true, I want them never to fall, want them to twist
     so tightly into their spins they break

out of being, combust

     into nothing, presto—   shifting grains
of gold dust.

IV

But they have all the duende God gave a speed bump!

They're silly, these skaters. They're hopeless.

V

And if, finished, emerging from a routine, one of them
        should look contemplative   —if skating in, she should drop

her gaze, hands on her hips, her face long

like a woman looking for seashells, or if one sits on the bench

terrifically skittery, waiting for scores, that's just more art.
        You can trust them

only when they're drifting to the center,
        before the music begins,

when they are leaving the pose of themselves
        for the pose of the routine, a blur

where they are going in—

VI

If then

Giant Snow Woman

A winter's entertainment we dreamed up
eight years ago, Olympia. A lark

yet she looms over the recreation center,
in the dark where she is white

as white is in a dream, in dream life

though she is real, Olympia: expected yet sudden,
like pansies in flowerboxes in spring, but huge—

She is packed in, smoothed, she is made specific
by our donations: evergreens are her arms that reach;

her apron's someone's tattered tent; and the tips
of skis, plunged in, are lashes. How they curl,

Olympia, and how she smiles

as if we circled her still with wolf-whistles,
with plastic cups of wine, with our silly singing—

As if, like ponies gathered at a fence,

we stood stamping our cold feet
on the cold ground: *Ho, Ho. Hey, Olympia*—

But she is a Giant Snow Woman!
She does not blink;

until knocked over, dismantled in the parking lot,
she is open, awake, her eyes

straight-forward, as a stop-light stuck on red,
swayed by wind, in the center of town, Olympia.

Private Plane

So that one sees the world calmly,
Finally, as the pilot does—

Nightly, and each town appears, still in place, its passages
Evident after the fact, and clear and commanding
As emergency lighting.

    Where were you there? And of
The lights one passes over a few
Surge eagerly, hopelessly, someone

Very shy, at the edge of speech—
So that, eventually, the towns drift back

And one moves on, over woods, a farm, an empty field
        (slow slope and blue-washed)

Freed now from all of that: groundless
And alone in the clear, as at the exact moment

A parent dies (except then
Inside, one feels a bit wild-eyed).

Ruins in Sunlight

Up the side of the hill
The house is a lace of stones

A few grown over with earth
And a few smooth
And ridged, as molars

What was yard, sunlight now,
An expanse of grass—

And the stones
Forming the ruined house

Are worse than a map:
Allocation of rooms,

Divisions, architecture—

Nothing, it turns out, was
Secret, or private

Lines

An e-mail Mary sent: *Like all aligned*

If only therefore one person

To an over-all black translucency

She said, the better to, the better to

Once inside the dark theater

Effervescent, this mountain light

I wanted to remain vision only

Be careful with that match!

The Big Hopeless

Here it comes again, the Big Hopeless, each time

but I keep walking through Rittenhouse—the drunks

sacked out there—along Jewelry Row, the shops
locked-up, each display case blue, bare
     and alarmed

And here it comes again, Big Hopeless, an opening
in the city drawing litter down the street

slowly, in the middle of the night, while air conditioners
     hum across town, while they drip into sidewalks

—I'm telling you I didn't know, I did not know
we had longings so great
until it was too late:

they grew bright only when imagined
     like a line of taxis at a taxi stand.

Arson

I remember horses, trees,
A house in the window.
My mother's heart
Was the sketch of a stove,

Then wide as a new idea,
The feeling God gave her.
When you left me
I could not contain it,

Could not believe
The Datsun's cracked windshield
Was reasonable.
Did you? The trees

Hung down their branches
And sunlight ran
Into that body,
Straight in—

Then I believed.

Dunes

(Red Desert, Wyoming)

In position they shift
Holding the little rain in. They are still, busy, like the mind
As the mind sleeps.

All that we saw, driving there—wildlife
Made us slow, the air conditioning up high

Four ponies
Descending a hill, an eagle on a telephone pole,
The jackrabbit vanished into sage brush

But never existed really for us, like reflections
Crossing in a window (the teenage girls
Drift through your haircut): a burrowing owl,

A sunset streaking the motel

Where we'd returned, where we'd gone
Back to bed, and afterwards
You recited *Sailing to Byzantium*

And I shut my eyes to see, along with you
The bird, the tree, the gold enameling.

Delphinium

You see they are not silent

Like a row of windows at twilight
Or a circle of charred wood, stones

You see like dreams they are private
No matter the traffic the descriptions

Though iridescent between hedge and pine
Upright in the garden

They never will mirror you
Only absorb you

Only send back this blue
Perfectly still, and as strict

As a note held
Back in the throat

Rising beyond the body,
So what you hear in the garden

You later will hear inside
At night in your own voice

I am awake   Do not touch me
I will be awake all night

Acknowledgments & Notes

Grateful acknowledgement is made to the editors of the journals in which these poems first appeared:

AGNI: "Private Plane" and "Cat"
The American Poetry Review: "Dunes," "Ruins in Sunlight," "In the Snow," "Night Snow" and "Aspens"
Borderlands: excerpts of "Detail"
Country Dog Review: "Skating"
Iron Horse Literary Review: "Night"
Raritan: "Clean Houses," "Night Drive," and "Delphinium"
The Massachusetts Review: "Winter Prairie"
Think Journal: "Caldera" and "The Big Hopeless"
Zone 3: "Iowa," "Arson," and "Lake in Moonlight"
32 Poems: "Evening"

"The Film" appears on *From the Fishouse* (www.fishousepoems.org) and in *From the Fishouse* (Persea Books, 2009).

"Winter Prairie" and "Night Drive" appear also in *Poets of the American West* (Many Voices Press, 2010).

*

Lines 3 and 8 of "Lines" are taken from Elizabeth Bishop's "The Filling Station." The second sections on pages 38 and 40 are taken from Theodore Roethke's "Moss Gathering."

*

The writing of this book was generously supported by the UCross Foundation, Caldera, the Baltic Center for Writers and Translators, the Pennsylvania Council on the Arts, West Chester University, Alex Long, Jane Hilberry, Julia Levine, Chez Julie Nathanielsz, and the University of Wyoming. I am particularly grateful to Beth Loffreda, Director of the University of Wyoming MFA in Creative Writing and entirely excellent friend. My enduring gratitude to H.L. Hix, for his response to this work and for his company, beyond compare.

Thank you to Dinah Fried and Rita Lascaro. Thank you to Persea Books, especially to Michael and Karen Braziller. Especially to Gabe.

About the Author

H.L.HIX

KATE NORTHROP is the author of *Back Through Interruption* and *Things Are Disappearing Here*, a *New York Times Book Review* "Editor's Choice" and finalist for the James Laughlin Award. She teaches at the University of Wyoming and lives in Laramie.